Capriccio Espagnol

and Other Concert Favorites
in Full Score

Nikolay
RIMSKY-KORSAKOV

DOVER PUBLICATIONS, INC.
Mineola, New York

Copyright

Copyright © 1998 by Dover Publications, Inc.
All rights reserved under Pan American and International Copyright Conventions.

Published in Canada by General Publishing Company, Ltd., 30 Lesmill Road, Don Mills, Toronto, Ontario.
Published in the United Kingdom by Constable and Company, Ltd., 3 The Lanchesters, 162–164 Fulham Palace Road, London W6 9ER.

Bibliographical Note

This Dover edition, first published in 1998, is a new compilation of three works originally published separately in early, authoritative editions, n.d. Notes and lists of contents and instrumentation are newly added.

International Standard Book Number: 0-486-40249-5

Manufactured in the United States of America
Dover Publications, Inc., 31 East 2nd Street, Mineola, N.Y. 11501

CONTENTS

Dance of the Buffoons

From Act III of *Snow Maiden (Snegurochka)*,
an opera in a prologue and four acts
(1877–82)

Music by
NIKOLAY RIMSKY-KORSAKOV

Libretto by the composer,
based on the play by Aleksandr Ostrovsky
(1873)

INSTRUMENTATION

Piccolo [Flauto piccolo, Picc.]
2 Flutes [Flauti, Fl.]
2 Oboes [Oboi, Ob.]
2 Clarinets in B♭ ("B") [Clarinetti, Cl.]
2 Bassoons [Fagotti, Fg.]

4 Horns in F [Corni, Cor.]
2 Trumpets in B♭ ("B") [Trombe, Tr.]
3 Trombones [Tromboni, Trb(e).]
Tuba [Tub(a), T.]

Timpani [Timp(ani), Tp.]

Percussion
  Triangle [Triang(olo), Trg., Tg., T.]
  Tambourine [Tamburino, Tb.]
  Cymbals and Bass Drum
    [Piatti e (u.) Cassa, P. e C.]

Violins I, II [Violini, Viol.]
Violas [Viole]
Cellos [Violoncelli, Vc.]
Basses [Contrabassi, C.B.]

2

Dance of the Buffoons

(1877–82)

Dance of the Buffoons 13

14   *Dance of the Buffoons*

Dance of the Buffoons

Dance of the Buffoons

28   *Dance of the Buffoons*

Capriccio Espagnol

(Kaprichchio na ispanskiye temï)

Op. 34 (1887)

Based on a projected Fantasia on Spanish themes
for violin and orchestra

INSTRUMENTATION

Piccolo [Flauto piccolo, Picc.]
2 Flutes [Flauti, Fl.]
2 Oboes [Oboi, Ob.]
English Horn [Corno inglese]
2 Clarinets in A, B♭ ("B") [Clarinetti, Clar.]
2 Bassoons [Fagotti, Fag.]

4 Horns in F [Corni, Cor.]
2 Trumpets in A, B♭ ("B") [Trombe, Tr.]
3 Trombones [Tromboni, Trb(e).]
Tuba [Tub(a), T.]

Timpani [Timpani/o, Timp.]

Percussion

    Castanets [Castagnetti, Cast.]
    Triangle [Triang(olo), Trg., Tg., T.]
    Tambourine [Tamburino, Tamb.]
    Snare Drum [Tamburo milit(aire), Tamb.]
    Cymbals [Piatti]
    Bass Drum [Cassa]

Harp [Arpa]

Violins I, II [Violini, Viol.]
Violas [Viole]
Cellos [Violoncelli, Vcell., V.C.]
Basses [Contrabassi, C. Bass]

Capriccio Espagnol

Op. 34 (1887)

I. Alborada

Vivo e strepitoso. M.M. ♩=126

Vivo e strepitoso.

II. Variazioni

41

Tempo I.

III. Alborado
[reprise]

IV. Scena e canto gitano

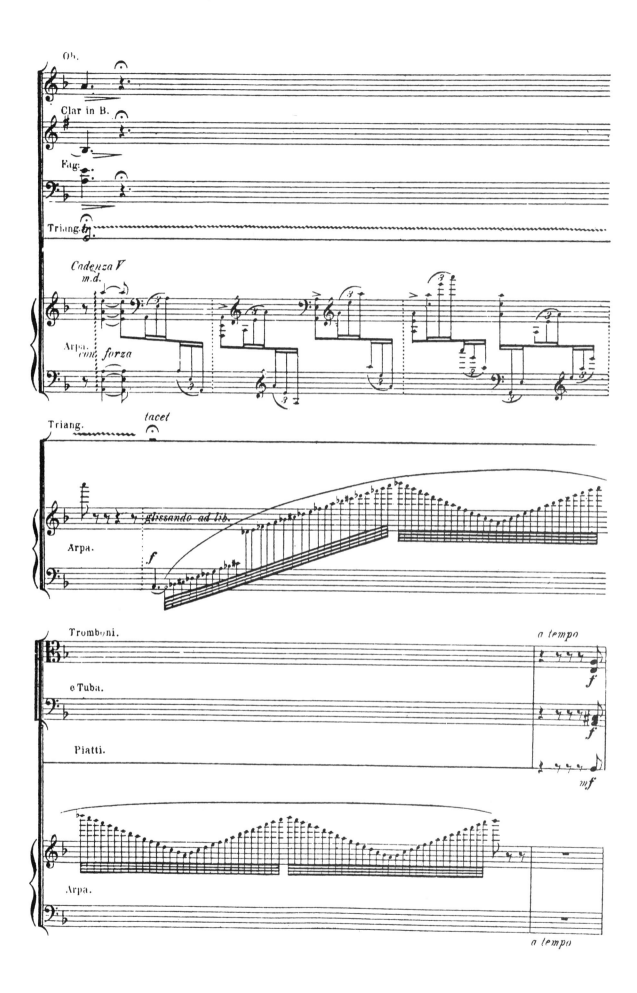

V. Fandango asturiano

To the memory of Moussorgsky and Borodin

Russian Easter Festival

(*Svetlïy prazdnik*—literally, "Serene Feast-day")

Overture

Op. 36 (1888)

Based on themes from the *Obikhod*,
a collection of Russian Orthodox canticles

INSTRUMENTATION

3 Flutes [Flauti, Fl.]
   Fl. III doubles Piccolo [Fl(auto) picc(olo)]
2 Oboes [Oboi, Ob.]
2 Clarinets in C [Clarinetti, Cl.]
2 Bassoons [Fagotti, Fg.]

4 Horns in F [Corni, Cor.]
2 Trumpets in A, B♭ ("B") [Trombe, Tbe.]
3 Trombones [Tromboni, Tbni/e.]
Tuba

Timpani [Timp.]

Percussion

   Tubular Bells [Campanelli, Camp.]
     (or Glockenspiel)
   Triangle [Triangolo, Trgl.]
   Cymbals [Piatti]
   Bass Drum [Cassa]
   Tamtam [Tamt., Tam.]

Harp [Arpa]

Violins I [Violini, Vl.] (20–12 players)
Violins II [Violini, Vl.] (18–10)
Violas [Viola, Vle.] (14–8)
Cellos [Violoncelli, Vc.] (12–8)
Basses [Contra Bassi, Cb.] (10–6)

"It was this legendary and pagan side of the holiday—this transition from the bleak, strange evening of Passion Saturday to the unleashed pagan-religious merrymaking of Easter Sunday morn— that I wanted to express in my Overture."

Nikolay Rimsky-Korsakov
Freely translated from
Chronicle of My Musical Life, 1909

COMPOSER'S PROGRAMME

Let God arise, let his enemies be scattered: let them also that hate him flee before him.

As smoke is driven away, so drive them away: as wax melteth before the fire, so let the wicked perish at the presence of God.

Psalm 68

And when the sabbath was past, Mary Magdalene, and Mary the mother of James, and Salome, had bought sweet spices, that they might come and anoint him.

And very early in the morning the first day of the week, they came unto the sepulchre at the rising of the sun.

And they said among themselves, Who shall roll us away the stone from the door of the sepulchre?

And when they looked, they saw that the stone was rolled away: for it was very great.

And entering into the sepulchre, they saw a young man sitting on the right side, clothed in a long white garment; and they were affrighted.

And he saith unto them, Be not affrighted: Ye seek Jesus of Nazareth, which was crucified: he is risen.

The Gospel According to St. Mark: xvi, 1-6

The joyous news spread throughout the universe and those who hated him fled before him and disappeared as smoke.

"Resurrexit" sang the angel choirs in heaven, to the sound of archangel trumpets and the whir of seraphim wings.

"Resurrexit" sang the priests in the temples in the midst of incense clouds and of the light of innumerable candles and the carillon of triumphant bells.

Russian Easter Festival
Overture
Op. 36 (1888)

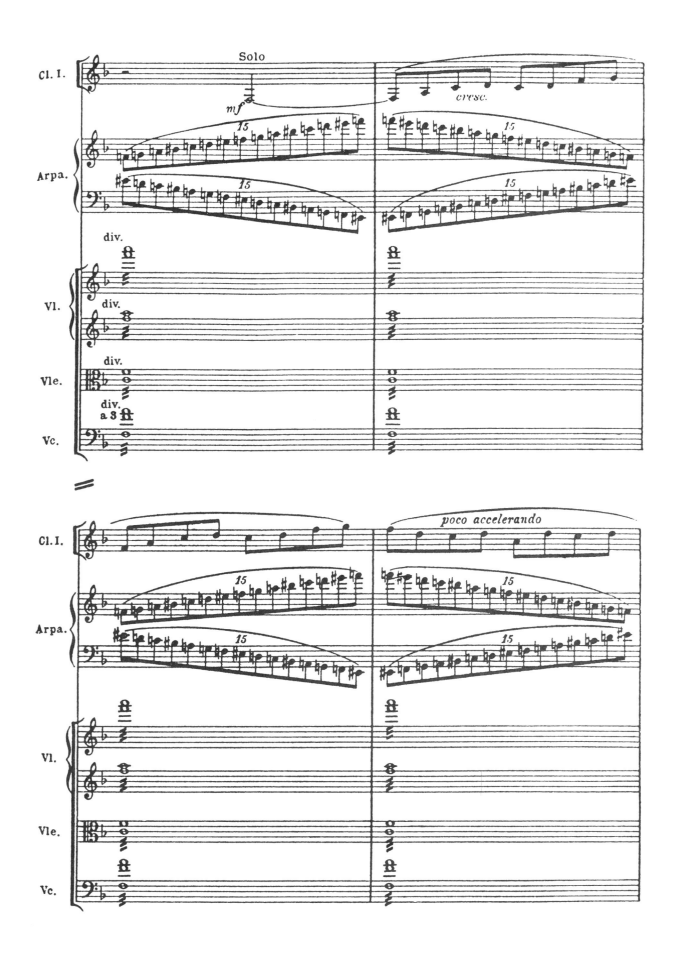

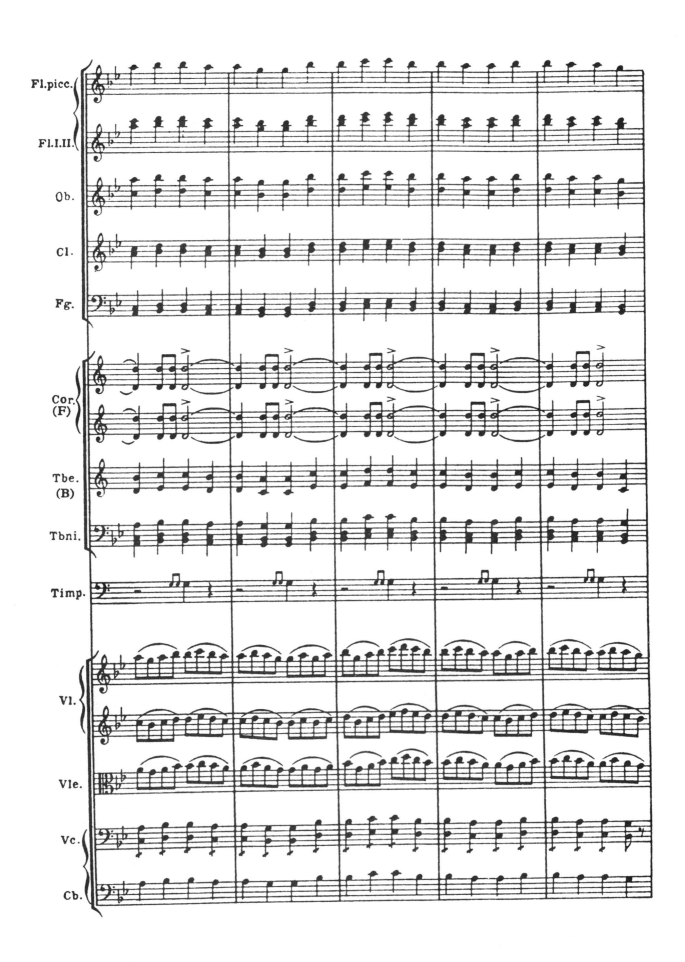

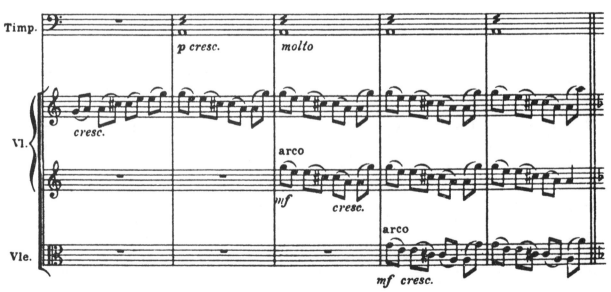

END OF EDITION